Music Minus One Vocals

BIG BAND Female Standards

songs in the style of
LINDA RONSTADT

2184

BIG BAND Female Standards

songs in the style of
LINDA RONSTADT

CONTENTS

ISBN 978-1-941566-60-2

What's New

Words by Johnny Burke
Music by Bob Haggart

Crazy He Calls Me

Music by Carl Sigman
Lyrics by Bob Russell

Lover Man
(OH, WHERE CAN YOU BE?)

By Jimmy Davis, Roger Ramirez
and Jimmy Sherman

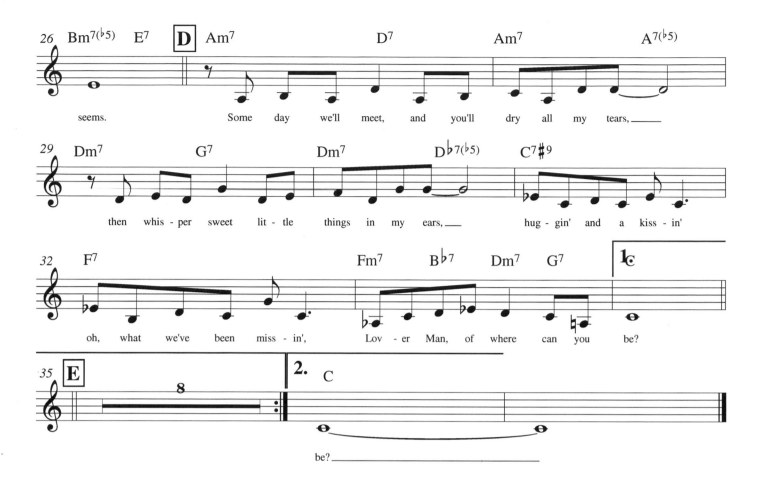

When I Fall In Love
from ONE MINUTE TO ZERO

Words by Edward Heyman
Music by Victor Young

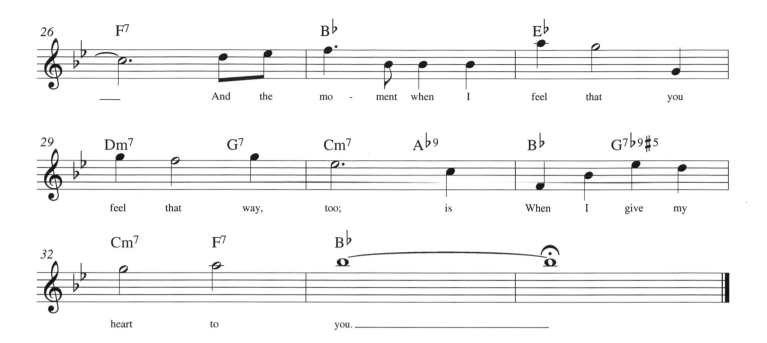

And the mo - ment when I feel that you

feel that way, too; is When I give my

heart to you.

Skylark

Words and Music by
Johnny Mercer and Hoagy Carmichael

Mean To Me

Words and Music by
FRED AHLERT and ROY TURK

14

You Took Advantage Of Me

from PRESENT ARMS

Words by Lorenz Hart
Music by Richard Rodgers

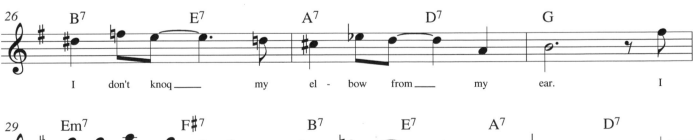

Sophisticated Lady

Words and Music by Duke Ellington,
Irving Mills and Mitchell Parish

Day In, Day Out

Music by Rube Bloom
Lyric by Johnny Mercer

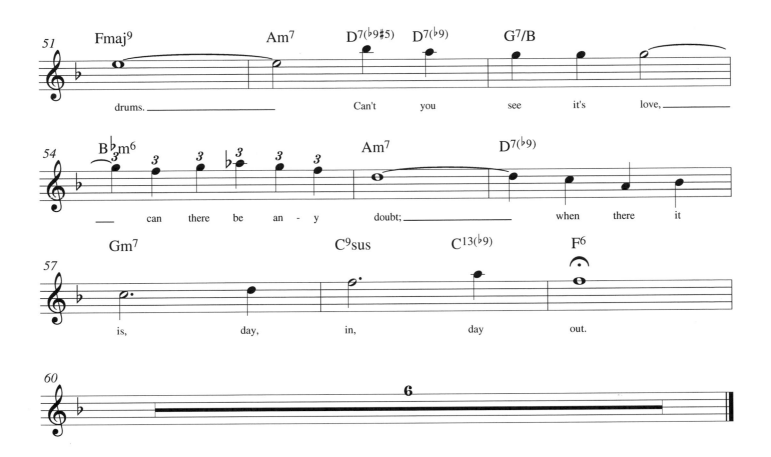

Fmaj⁹ ... Am⁷ ... D⁷⁽♭⁹♯⁵⁾ D⁷⁽♭⁹⁾ ... G⁷/B

drums. _____ Can't you see it's love, _____

B♭m⁶ ... Am⁷ ... D⁷⁽♭⁹⁾

_____ can there be an-y doubt; _____ when there it

Gm⁷ ... C⁹sus ... C¹³⁽♭⁹⁾ ... F⁶

is, day, in, day out.

Bewitched, Bothered and Bewildered

from PAL JOEY

Words by Lorenz Hart
Music by Richard Rodgers

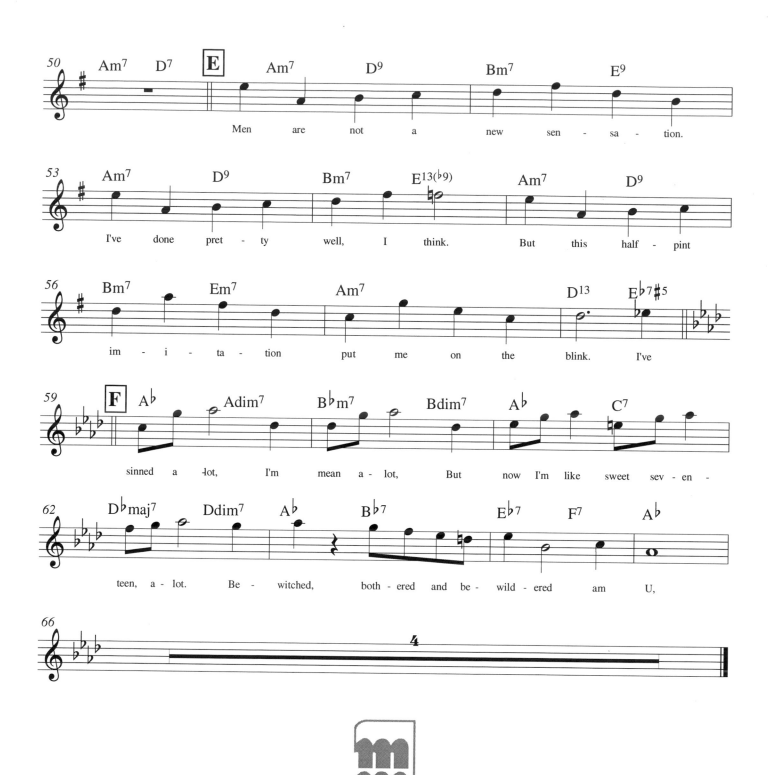

Music Minus One
50 Executive Boulevard • Elmsford, New York 10523–1325
914–592–1188 • e-mail: info@musicminusone.com
www.musicminusone.com

MMO 2184

ISBN 978-1-941566-60-2